This book is dedicated to my dad,
Joseph Lappi
(also known as "Pappy Joe")

My dad was always my #1 supporter
of Blood Brother Farms.
He loved to visit any chance he got!

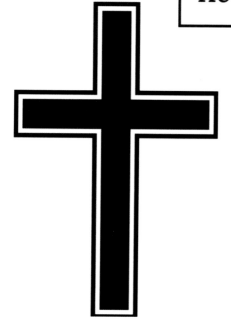

*The journey I go on is one
that my father paved
before me. I wouldn't be
anywhere without him and
I miss him dearly.*

Blood Brother Farms

Money Down Productions

Farms

"It Started with one egg"

Chickens need a place to live. So before you decide to get any, be sure you have a coop! Make sure your coop is off of the ground and built well! It's very important to keep us out of the harsh weather, especially during winter! We don't like the wind or snow very much. Keeping us out of the cold wind at night will help us to lay more eggs and be happy and healthy!

Oh, and remember to always shut our door at night, we don't want a fox to hurt us!

TOP SHELF EGGS

BLOOD BROTHER FARMS

Chickens don't need much, but there ARE a couple things we need in order to grow and be happy and healthy! Chickens really like straw! We love when the Chicken Farmer gives us brand new straw to lay our eggs and to also rest in after our morning breakfast! We also love to eat! We will gladly eat all the bugs in your yard but we also need some feed from the store. We prefer local feed and this can found at your feed mills .

TOP SHELF EGGS

BLOOD BROTHER FARMS

This is where we take a break and get some water! Here at the farm, it's not just important to have fresh food for our bellies, but we also need fresh water everyday! Every morning when we get our breakfast, our farmer gives us new water. We drink a lot of water in the summer so always make sure you keep a close eye on our water bowl!

TOP SHELF EGGS

BLOOD BROTHER FARMS

Okay Chicken Farmer Trainees, I think I see the Chicken Farmer walking in the barn, let's go see if he's collecting eggs.

TOP SHELF EGGS

BLOOD BROTHER FARMS

Wow! This looks like an impressive group of trainees! Donald told me about you and said you guys are almost ready to have your own chickens! As a Chicken Farmer, you have to go out and collect your eggs everyday! You don't want them to crack in the barn or freeze in the winter! A good Chicken Farmer will check on the eggs a couple times a day! Just this afternoon, we collected a basketful. By the way, does anyone know how a chick is hatched?

TOP SHELF
EGGS

BLOOD BROTHER FARMS

Before a good Chicken Farmer goes in for the night, you have to make sure you close all the doors to the coops! You don't want any predators to hurt your chickens!

Well, you all did great today! You are now officially Chicken Farmers! Now, go build a coop and get some chickens. Remember, always be nice to your animals, they are counting on you!!

TOP SHELF EGGS

BLOOD BROTHER FARMS

This is Bethel, she's been laying on her eggs for 16 days now! For an egg to become a chick, the mom has to decide that she wants to sit on her eggs for 21 days rather than have the farmer collect them daily. After 21 days, the chicks will begin to hatch! The mother hen needs to help raise the chicks until they can be out in the weather! For about 8 weeks, the mother hen will protect her chicks and keep them warm and safe.
I think it's time for us to go close the coop doors for the night!

TOP SHELF EGGS

BLOOD BROTHER FARMS

ABOUT US...

What started innocently with 6 hens and a Rooster named "Donald", has led us here.

Averaging between 100-125 birds for our farm fresh egg sales, consistently raising various age groups of chickens for public sale, an annual Easter Hatch of chicks, farm apparel and our own, one-of-a-kind, Specialty Grade Breakfast Blend Coffee, we became an official business in 2023 shortly after getting married.

LOCATED IN:
ASHVILLE, PA
EST. 2020

Our family...

Our small chicken farm is not short of farm hands to say the least!

We've been blessed with raising 3 children while we chase our dreams.

Our kids are: Ethan (11), Grace (6) and Savannah (5), you could definitely say we have our hands full!

The kiddos are also accompanied by our two farm "Security" dogs.

Our dogs are: Boomer, he is a Blue Tick Beagle, and Nova, she's our 1 year old Dalmatian.

Our goals...

Our main focus is providing "Top Shelf" products from our farm fresh eggs to our coffee!

If it has our name on it then you can guarantee there were no short cuts when producing your goods.

We want you to rely on us to get your morning started right, by having our quality products, and as we like to say "Fuel for the farmer".

We take pride in our Customer Service, from every order to every conversation, it is our mission to sustain the absolute best service possible to all!

As always, we thank you for all of your support!

PLEASE FOLLOW US ON OUR SOCIAL MEDIAS; (FACEBOOK, INSTAGRAM, TIKTOK @BLOODBROTHERFARMS) TO KEEP UP WITH OUR NEWEST PRODUCTS WE CREATE OR SALE HERE LOCALLY! THANK YOU ONCE AGAIN FROM OUR ENTIRE FAMILY!

"THE ONLY GOALS YOU DON'T GRAB, ARE THE ONES YOU STOP REACHING FOR"

Good Morning Farmers in Training!

When the rooster crows, it's time to Chicken Farm!

But first, we need to teach you what life on a chicken farm is all about.

And, lucky for you we have the best teacher possible.

Let me introduce you to our ROOSTER, DONALD!

Donald has been running the farm here for years.

He is so excited to take you on a tour and teach you all about chickens.

Donald will share with you everything you need to know so that you can go home and start your own chicken farm!

So pay attention farmers--your future chickens are counting on it !!

TOP SHELF
EGGS

BLOOD BROTHER FARMS

The fox
vs
The
Hound

Book #2
Coming
in 2024

TOP SHELF
EGGS

BLOOD BROTHER FARMS

The only goals you don't grab, are the ones you stop reaching for!

 Chicken Farmer

Made in the USA
Middletown, DE
11 March 2024

51297614R00015